FLORENCE

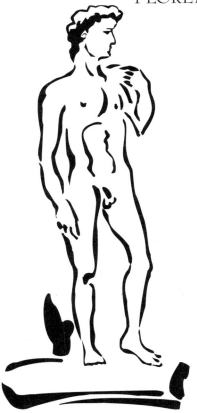

LYNN PORTNOY

Diamond Publishers

With sincere thanks to my editor, Judy Bobrow,
Lisa Hajnal of Grigg Graphic Services, Inc., and for all of
the tips from my American and Italian friends, particularly:
Liliana Aonzo, Susi Casolini, F. Frediano, Carol King,
Father N. Maestrini, Lora Vezzosi
and the late Geraldine Naditz.

A most grateful thanks to
Vivian Tonnino Gori, Patricia B. Smith and my
invaluable Italian language and arts editor.

Preface

The 21st century may be called the century of female explorers. After nearly two years of travel talks and book signings for *Going Like Lynn – Paris* and *Going Like Lynn – New York* (the first two books in a series of liberating travel guidebooks for women), I have chatted with an enormous number of savvy women travelers who have enthusiastically discussed and shared information on every aspect of travel. From these discussions I have discovered how eager women are to learn about different cultures and destinations as well as practical information involving safety, tipping, hotels and restaurants. The women that I met enjoy exploring every nook and cranny of a city and discovering off-the-beaten-path sightseeing as well as great shopping. They told me they loved feeling like insiders even on a first visit and appreciated information told from a women's viewpoint.

In *Going Like Lynn – Florence*, I invite my "insider readers" to join me in the pleasure of meandering the narrow medieval streets, bridges and piazzas of this fascinating city – visiting 21st-century cafés and boutiques as well as magnificent art treasures from the Renaissance. Pick and choose from my suggestions and whatever you decide to do, just enjoy Florence, using this book as a catalyst to ignite your own travel engine!

Lynn Portnoy

Table of Contents

Table of Contents

(continued)

You may have the universe if
I may have Italy.

-Giuseppe Verdi

Why Florence?

Florence is a city that I know and love. It is female friendly, relatively safe and filled with countless Renaissance treasures in a setting of timeless beauty. Built along the Arno River, surrounded by rolling hills and cypress trees, it is a splendid tableau that takes your breath away – particularly at dawn or dusk.

As a University of Michigan student more than 40 years ago, I was fortunate to study Renaissance art with Professor Marvin Eisenberg. He gave his students a lifelong appreciation and passion for the intellect and brilliance of this open-minded society out of which came masterpieces of architecture, painting, sculpture and literature, as well as many significant scientific discoveries.

In this guide, I share my love of the Renaissance culture and art of 14th- to 16th-century Florence, along with the earthly pleasures of 21st-century Florence, delicious Tuscan food and wine, interesting shopping and great walks and views. Best of all, you don't have to be a historian or art connoisseur to be enriched by this city. Just take time to get away from the crowds and walk up in the hills or along the banks of the Arno and let Florence work its magic on you.

"Buon Viaggio"
(Happy Travels)

Lynn Portnoy

Pre-Planning

For those who have read *Going Like Lynn – Paris*
and *Going Like Lynn – New York,* much of this
information is already second nature to you.

List in a small wallet-size notebook:
(without your name, address or phone)

✔ Your credit card numbers including expiration date and national
and international phone numbers
to call if lost.

✔ Passport number, city and date
issued, date of expiration.

✔ Driver's license number.

✔ Health card number.

✔ Traveler's health and cancellation
insurance policy number and
emergency number to call.
(Can be purchased from a travel
agent or you can call *Access*
1-800-284-8300.)

✔ Your doctor's and dentist's names and phone numbers.

✔ Addresses and phone numbers of hotels where you will be staying.

✔ Travelers check numbers and denominations.

✔ All reservation and confirmation numbers (airline and train tickets, hotels with price quoted, museum reservations, etc.)

✔ Phone numbers and addresses of the nearest American Embassy or Consulate. In Florence, the **American Consulate phone number is: 055-239-8276.**

✔ Your list of "must see" shops, restaurants and museums.

✔ Name of close relative or friend to call in case of emergency (who also should have copies of your itinerary as well as all of the above numbers, a copy of your passport and a passport photo.)

✔ Prescription, dosage and generic names of drugs that you take and eyeglass or contact lenses prescription as well as allergies to foods and drugs.

Pre-Planning Essentials

An extra passport photo and, if you have one, an expired passport. Keep these in your lingerie or cosmetic bag.

Three copies of your passport, one for your make-up or lingerie case, one for your purse and one for a friend or relative.

Purchase airline tickets after checking prices with a travel agent, airlines, the internet and the Sunday *New York Times* travel section for airline jobbers advertising cheap tickets.

Book hotels (for details see Hotel chapter). Many travelers now book on the internet. Just remember that what you are seeing is a biased statement from the hotel. Others use the airlines' hotels. These are usually large impersonal tour group hotels. I like to talk to friends or read articles and small hotel guidebooks in which people personally recommend a small hotel and tell you why.

Pre-Planning Essentials, continued...

Book other transportation, such as train tickets or car rental.

Order Italian currency called lira (plural, lire) or after January 1, 2002, the European currency called Euros, and purchase travelers checks. The amount is up to you. (I charge my hotels, most meals and my few purchases.) Contact your local bank or order by phone, 1-888-CHASE84, or on line, www.currencytogo.com, from Chase-Manhattan Bank. Orders are delivered within 24 hours. There is a small fee for orders under $500 and everything can be charged to your credit card. You also can change money in Florence at Bancomats (ATMs) as well as at banks and American Express.

Bring two different credit cards. Make sure you have a least $1,500 credit available on each card. (If one is lost, you will have a second card in the hotel safe, along with your passport and travelers checks.)

Pre-Planning Essentials, continued...

You can use your passport photo-copy to change money so your passport can stay in the hotel safe.

Read guidebooks, travel articles and talk to friends for their suggestions of favorite places, museums, shops and restaurants.

For super obsessive-compulsives like me, copy the same information on two index cards. Keep one copy in your cosmetic bag and one in your lingerie case with an extra passport photo so if your purse is stolen or lost you have complete copies.

Order museum tickets for Uffizi, Accademia, Pitti and Medici Chapel at 011-39-055-294-883 as soon as you know your travel dates. This saves hours of standing in line.

Lightweight, simple,
packable separates in solids
or subtle tweeds that can be
layered, are seasonless and
can be dressed up or down
with accessories.

Wardrobe in a Bag

Florence is a small conservative northern city. The Florentines are elegant and well dressed, wearing smart suits, great shoes, handbags and leather gloves in the fall and early spring. Tourists wearing their jogging outfits, shorts, sneakers and printed T-shirts generally stand out like sore thumbs.

My *Going Like Lynn Wardrobe in a Bag* catalog includes lightweight, simple, packable separates in solids or subtle tweeds that can be layered, are seasonless and can be dressed up or down with accessories.

Here are a few tips:

- I pack old oversized T-shirts for sleeping that I can give away to hotel staff or to the American Church to make room for a few purchases.

- I travel with one pair of old shoes that I can wear in the rain and also give away if wearable (again making room for another purchase).

11

- My perfect lightweight, fold-up hooded raincoat doubles as my bathrobe. (I often have room service breakfast and need a robe.)

- I always have one really elegant understated suit with me that I feel great in and can wear for any occasion with a change of accessories as well as one pair of good shoes and a decent bag.

If you are checking your bag here is a list of essentials for your purse, which is really a carry-on tote bag:

A plastic bag with:

- A change of underwear.

- A T-shirt or lightweight sweater.

- A pair of loose socks to wear as slippers.

- A sleep mask.

- A small cosmetic bag – with mini-size compact, lipstick, hairbrush, soap, toothbrush, mouthwash, toothpaste, moisturizer, medications*, deodorant

and half of an old washcloth or anything else that will help revive you
after traveling all night or if your luggage is lost.*(Prescription medications
must be properly labeled and include
the generic name. Your pharmacist can
put them in small vials for you. Take
enough for an extra week in case you
get stranded for a few days due to a
strike or other unforeseen circum-
stance. Prescription drugs must
always be with you, never in your
checked luggage.)

- I suggest a good lightweight fabric
  purse with a shoulder strap and
  inside, two coin purses – one with $100
  American money, one credit card and
  a driver's license; the other with your
  passport, Italian lire or Euros and
  another credit card and museum
  reservation numbers.

Reading material such as:

- A tiny Italian translation book,
  like Berlitz.

- *Going Like Lynn – Florence.*

- A guidebook or page copies on
  the art and history of Florence
  (see Resources chapter).

- Paperback novel.

- Your purse notebook, traveler's insurance policy and travelers checks, hotel brochures and tickets (train and plane).

Wear your heaviest clothing on the plane:

- Lightweight raincoat with wide armholes.

- Blazer, wool jacket or summer-weight jacket.

- Long sleeve cotton T-shirt.

- Pants with elastic waist.

- Loose socks and sturdy dark walking shoes.

- Comfortable underwear – not tight or binding.

- Optional: a Pashmina (real or faux) shawl over your jacket is handy when the plane gets colder in mid-flight.

For photos of

Going Like Lynn Wardrobe In A Bag,

check my website, goinglikelynn.com or

call 1-888-386-9688 for our catalog.

We sell the wardrobe and the bag

minus lingerie, shoes and cosmetics.

ESSENTIALS TO PACK
FOR 10–12 DAYS

Nine Tops – Solid Colors

- Three cotton T-shirts or sweaters.
- One short sleeved or sleeveless silk shell.
- Two long sleeved silk sweaters.
- One wool or cashmere sweater.
- One silk, cashmere or Merino cardigan.
- One extra large, long T-shirt for sleeping.

Four Bottoms

- One solid dark pant in lightweight fabric, i.e., cotton, wool knit, gabardine or a synthetic blend.
- One solid colored dark street skirt, lightweight wool, synthetic blend or cotton.
- One dark solid soft pant or long skirt that doesn't wrinkle and can be worn day or evening.
- Another light cotton, synthetic or wool casual trousers for every day.

One Suit With Jacket

One dark pant or skirt suit to be
dressed up or down with accessories – could be lightweight wool,
synthetic or knit.

Underwear

Three sets plus two pair lightweight socks to wear with your
dark walking shoes.

Accessories

- One Pashmina real or faux shawl
  (if you are not wearing it on
  the plane).

- Two scarves or shawls – to dress
  up pant suit or jersey skirt or
  pants and silk sweater.

- One string faux pearls and
  earrings.

- One faux gold or silver pin
  and earrings or necklace
  and earrings

- One small flat purse to wear for
  dinner (pack your costume jewelry in it). I carry mine inside my
  tote bag on the plane.

Toiletries and Cosmetics

- One medium size toiletry case with miniature samples of mouth-wash, creams, lotions, toothpaste, two small toothbrushes, over-the-counter medications only – in small bottles. (Your prescription drugs are never in your luggage.)

- One make-up case – again, shop for smaller size products and take only what you really use every day.

NOTE: It is better to take two small items than one large. You can throw away the finished tooth-paste, cream, etc.

Footwear

- One pair comfortable low-heeled or flat shoes (dressier than your dark walking shoes) to wear when shopping and going out to a nice restaurant for lunch. (This could be the old giveaway pair.)

- One pair good, medium or low-heeled dressier pumps for dinner.

Optional: One pair lightweight sandals if late spring or early fall (or buy them in Italy where they are sold everywhere).

For photos of *Going Like Lynn Wardrobe In A Bag,* check my website, goinglikelynn.com or call 1-888-386-9688 for our catalog. We sell the wardrobe and the bag minus lingerie, shoes and cosmetics.

General Essentials

- Wear modest clothes when visiting churches – no shorts, bare midriffs or bare shoulders.

- If you don't want to stand out instantly as an American tourist, leave the white sneakers at home and keep your water bottle in your tote bag. (There are cafés all over Florence where you can stop, sit and have a half bottle of water for about $1 and enjoy the free entertainment of the local street scene as well as resting your feet.)

- Be patient (take deep breaths and count to ten). Italy is not always the most efficient country and sometimes can be a bit frustrating for a traveler.

- Be prepared for strikes that involve planes, trains, bus and baggage handlers – they are common all over Europe today. Go with the flow and somehow you will get where you are going and be glad you were traveling with one bag.

- Commercial street addresses on building walls in Florence end in a red lowercase "r." A black uppercase "R" indicates a residential address.

- Street names often change every few blocks. Always have a good map with you as well as your hotel card.

- Museum and church hours and fees change constantly. Check at the tourist office or have your hotel call.

- In Italy, it is still a good idea to carry small packages of tissue in your purse. Many public restrooms seem to be permanently out of toilet paper.

- Buy bus tickets at tobacco shops or the Central Bus Station near S. Maria Novella Church.

- Before your trip, buy an Italian language tape to listen to in your car, while dressing, etc.; it really helps. Learn a few useful Italian expressions or buy a small Italian phrase book to keep in your purse.

Tipping:

General: In the north, the tip is generally included in restaurant and hotel bills; but if you had good service, leave the equivalent of $1 - $2 (at 2,000 lire to a dollar, it would be 2,000 to 4,000 lire per person). If not included, 10 percent is standard.

Taxis: Long distances or airports and stations with luggage – 10 percent. Short distances – 5 percent (or 1,000 or 2,000 lire).

Hotels: Concierge or front desk staff only if they made reservations, gave directions or provided any special services. If there are several front desk personnel that assisted you, leave an envelope with your thanks, name and room number. The amount depends on how many extra services they provided, how many days you used their service and the price of the hotel. (Leave approximately $2-$5 a day or 4,000 to 10,000 lire.) If only one particular person assisted you, just give that person $5 - $10 (10,000 - 20,000 lire). Tip maids $1 a day (2,000 lire) per person.

- An absolutely essential sentence: "**NON PARLO ITALIANO – PARLA INGLESE?**" ("*I don't speak Italian – do you speak English?*")

- If making many purchases, **American-owned Mailboxes ETC** on Via della Scala 13r, 055-268-173, will send your things home by UPS or Federal Express within seven working days. Expensive but efficient. (Many women send home their old clothes. You must have your purchases, receipts and tax refund forms with you when leaving Europe so you can have your tax refund forms stamped. Remember to do this before checking in at the airport for your flight to the U.S.)

- When arriving in the U.S., DO NOT LIE TO CUSTOMS about the amount of purchases with you. The duty is nominal and not worth a hefty fine or jail sentence. Keep your receipts handy.

Favorite Charming Small Hotels

Florence has dozens of hotels of varying size, price and location. I asked several friends who visit Florence regularly for the names of their favorite hotels and had as many different responses. The following suggestions are my personal choices. For a wider variety, consult the general guidebooks listed in the Resource chapter or books listing hotels such as:

- *Small Charming Hotel Guide – Italy,* a Duncan Petersen Guide

- *Karen Brown's Italy Bed and Breakfasts*

- *Hotels and Country Inns of Character and Charm in Italy,* Fodor's Rivages

- *Italian Country Hideaways,* by Universe Press

Note: To call Florence from the U.S., remember to dial 011-39 before the phone number.

NORTHWEST SIDE OF ARNO RIVER
Near the American Consulate
and the Concert Hall

*I personally like this location because
of the wonderful views across the Arno River.
It is in an upscale Florentine neighborhood
and you can walk anywhere in 15 to
25 minutes or use the nearby bus stop
and taxi stand.*

**ARIELE, Via Magenta 11, 50123
Firenze, Phone: 055-211-509, Fax: 055-
268-521, Email: hotel.ariele@libero.it.
Rates: 170,000- 270,000 lire ($85-135),
doubles with breakfast and taxes.
Rooms: 40 with parking and garden.**
Near the concert hall, this old fashioned,
modest hotel is a good choice if you have
a car and great value if you are visiting in
spring through fall and can enjoy the lovely
garden. The plain bedrooms and baths are
adequate and vary in size, the staff is gracious and helpful. Only complaint from
guests: "Breakfast could be improved."

**HOTEL CASA DEL LAGO, Lungarno
A. Vespucci, 58, 50123 Firenze,
Phone: 055-216-141, Fax: 055-214-149,
Email: htlcasalago@tin.it. Rates:
160,000–230,000 lire ($85-$120).
Rooms: 17 – 10 with view.** Directly facing
the Arno is this newly renovated bed and
breakfast on the top floor of a small build-

ing. The view of the south side of Florence and the Arno River is priceless, particularly at dawn and dusk. The brand new rooms and bathrooms with showers are a terrific bargain. Try for one of the rooms with a view. There is a breakfast room but no sitting room or bar.

HOTEL CONSIGLI, Lungarno A. Vespucci 50, 50123 Firenze, Phone: 055-214-172, Fax: 055-219-367, Email: hconsigli@tin.it, Internet: www.hotelconsigli.com. Rates: 280,000 lire ($140) double, includes breakfast, tax and service. Rooms: 16.
In the same neighborhood overlooking the Arno River, this faded former mansion offers private parking. Sizes and furnishings vary in the old-fashioned bedrooms and baths. Try to book early for one of the vast rooms overlooking the Arno. The breakfast room has vaulted ceilings covered with frescoes. Don't miss the roof garden for the smashing view of the Arno and Florentine hills. It could make you want to paint! For the price, this is an old world find.

HOTEL PRINCIPE, Lungarno A. Vespucci, 34, 50123 Firenze, Phone: 055-284-848, Fax: 055-283-458, Email: hotel.principe@hotelprincipe.com, Internet: www.hotelprincipe.com, Rates: 275,000-510,000 lire ($140-$255), includes buffet breakfast, tax and service. Rooms: 20. This is my personal

favorite hotel. I enjoy the great service
and lots of little luxuries and comforts for
the price. The most unique feature, the
hotel-villa faces the Arno but has a lovely
large secret garden in the back. The garden, as well as the living room lounge bar,
is perfect for a quiet drink after a hectic
day of sightseeing. The Bronzi family
members are wonderful hosts with Anna
Bronzi, the elegant senior member, a true
Florentine treasure. During a recent visit I
met her while she was gardening. She took
the time to tell me wonderful stories about
her beautiful villa-hotel. Some of the
rooms have small terraces overlooking
either the Arno River or the beautiful
garden. The staff is professional and
extremely helpful. P.S. If they are full,
keep faxing or calling. They might get a
cancellation.

NORTH SIDE OF ARNO
HOTELS IN CENTER
*These hotels are only a stone's throw from
major monuments, museums and shopping.*

**TORNABUONI BEACCI,
Via Tornabuoni 3, 50123,
Phone: 055-212-645, Fax: 055-283-594,
Email: info@bhotel.it, Rates: 220,000-
400,000 lire ($110-$200). Rooms: 34.**
Located on the top floor of the 14th century palace, Minerbetti Strozzi. Take the ele-
vator down and you are in the midst of
every designer boutique – a true shopper's

paradise. The Beacci Tornabuoni has a lovely salon and rooftop garden along with comfortable bedrooms and baths. From March through September, they serve dinner at a modest price. A quiet elegant setting with a friendly staff in a super location, very popular with celebrities and politicians. Book early.

BRETAGNA, Lungarno Corsini 6, 50123 (Next to British Consulate), Phone: 055-289-618, Fax: 055-289-619, Email: hotelpens.bretagna@agora.stm.it, Rates: 110,000-195,000 lire ($55-$100) includes breakfast, taxes and service. Rooms: 18. Terrific location on the north side of the Arno. For under $100 (one bedroom has a view of the Arno River) this simple family-owned hotel on the top floor of a historic Florentine palace (Palazzo Gionfigliazzi) is a great bargain. The tiny rooms are functional and some have private baths, television and direct-dial telephones. There is a lovely view of the Arno from the living room window and a cozy dining room for breakfast. Last but not least, there is an elevator in the building and this hotel is only five minutes from the Ponte Vecchio.

MORANDI ALLA CROCETTA, Via Laura 50, 50121, Phone: 055-234-4747, Fax: 055-248-0954, Email: <u>welcome@hotelmorandi.it</u>, Internet: <u>www.hotelmorandi.it</u>. Rates: 200,000-330,000 lire ($105-$175). Rooms: 10. Breakfast extra. A charming upscale bed and breakfast next to the archeological museum in a residential neighborhood in the historic district. You are a guest in a private home of an English woman who settled here many years ago. The English-speaking concierges include Frank Peters who gives the excellent history tour of Florence (see Resources).

HOTEL MONNA LISA, Borgo Pinti 27, 50121, Phone: 055-247-9751, Fax: 055-247-9755, Internet: <u>www.monnalisa.it</u>, Email: <u>monnalis@ats.it</u>. Rates: 220,000-600,000 lire ($110-300). Rooms: 30. An elegant historic palace overflowing with charm. The bedrooms range from very small to extremely large and are furnished with many lovely antiques and oil paintings. There is a beautiful courtyard garden, a stunning living room, a cozy bar and an elegant breakfast room in a quiet oasis only a five minute walk from the Duomo. I found the staff friendly and the surroundings beautiful. If you can afford it, this is a great choice.

SOUTH SIDE OF ARNO RIVER

The next two lovely hotels, on the south side of the Arno River, are highly recommended for those preferring a quiet neighborhood.

**CLASSIC HOTEL,
Viale Machiavelli, 25, 50125 Firenze,
Phone: 055-229-351, Fax: 055-229-353,
Email: info@classichotel.it. Rates:
175,000-275,000 lire ($90-$140).
Rooms: 20.** Near the Boboli Gardens, in an elegant neighborhood, the Classic has a lovely small garden and an excellent, friendly staff. The house-hotel is homey, extremely comfortable, bright and cheerful. I think this is one of the best values for the price in Florence. Again, you are in a real neighborhood here, not in the main tourist frenzy. There are parking facilities and you can easily leave your car and take the convenient bus to the historic center in under 10 minutes or a 20-25 minute walk.

**HOTEL SILLA, Via de' Renai 5,
50125 Firenze, Phone: 055-234-2888,
Fax: 055-234-1437, Email: <u>hotelsilla@tin.it</u>,
Internet: <u>www.hotelsilla.it</u>.
Rates: About 210,000–290,000 lire
($105-$145). Rooms: 36.** In a medieval
quarter, on the south side of the Arno, is
this old-fashioned hotel that was originally
a 15th century palace. You are a short walk
across the bridge from S. Croce and en
route to the scenic climb up to S. Miniato
and about a 10 to 15 minute walk to both
the Pitti Palace and the north side historic
district. The bedrooms are plain but the
highlight is the gorgeous terrace for drinks
and breakfast. The bedrooms facing the
street or those on the top floor with a peek
of the Arno are larger, if a bit noisier.

*In Going Like Lynn – Florence, I have
personally visited my recommendations,
looked at various rooms, talked with the
concierges and guests. I have included
only small hotels in good locations with
friendly staff where women can feel safe
and comfortable.*

GENERAL TIPS
FOR ITALIAN HOTELS

- PRICES ARE SUBJECT TO CHANGE –
  please inquire when booking.

- If you are traveling alone and are
  claustrophobic, inquire about the
  cost of a double room for single
  use. The single rooms are usually
  the size of a cell.

- Many of the hotels charge the
  same for their better rooms
  (with city, river or garden views
  or larger rooms).

- I like to call the hotel to see how
  friendly the concierge is and ask
  questions about size of the room,
  the view and how quiet it is, how
  far from most sightseeing and,
  of course, the price. BE SURE TO
  REQUEST A BROCHURE OR A
  CARD. It takes weeks to receive
  mail from Italy – so call a few
  months ahead of your trip.

- If you need a quiet room, forget
  rooms with city or river views.
  They are usually facing the street
  and are noisier. Again, inquire
  when booking.

Restaurants

Inexpensive	$12 and under
Moderate	$10-$24
Expensive	$25 and up

NORTH SIDE

ACQUA AL DUE, Via della Vigna Vecchia 40r (between Via Isola delle Stinche and Via dell'Acqua) – Historic Center. Phone: 055-284-170. *Moderate.* It is well known for its assaggi (tastings), small servings of different types of pasta, salads, etc. as well as a full menu. The food is very good and the long communal tables create a party ambiance. Call ahead for reservations or be prepared to wait.

CANTINETTA ANTINORI, Piazza Antinori #3r – at the end of fashionable Via Tornabuoni. Phone: 055-292-234. *Expensive.* In the fabulous palace that houses the headquarters for Antinori Wines, this small sophisticated wine bar and restaurant is frequented at lunch by the local business and professional

community as well as tourists. I had
my lunch at the bar, sampling different
glasses of vino rosso with my beef carpaccio and artichoke lunch. The beautiful bar,
elegant setting, good food and wine makes
this a terrific choice for lunch, wine tasting or supper.

**i'PARIONE, Via del Parione 74/76r.
Phone: 055-214-005. Closed Tuesday.**
Moderate. This small charming restaurant
turns out scrumptious Tuscan specialties
and pastas. The gnocchi melt in your
mouth. Every dish I tried was delicious.
This is an excellent restaurant with an
interesting décor. I loved the contemporary murals as well as the table settings.

**NERBONE, Inside the Central Market
on the ground floor – behind San
Lorenzo Church. Phone: 055-219-949.
Monday – Sunday lunch. No Credit
Cards.** *Inexpensive.* An old Florentine
tradition. Stop as the locals do for a quick
snack or lunch at low prices. You might
be dining next to a Florentine aristocrat,
a market worker or an Asian visitor. Try
the daily specials as well as the traditional
Bollito (meat sandwich).

OSTERIA IL MOSTRINA, Via Borgognissanti 141r – close to Hotel Principe, Hotel Consigli and Casa del Lago. Phone: 055-239-8704. Closed Monday. *Inexpensive.* A good spot for a tasty Sunday supper. It is filled with neighborhood families so remember to reserve.

PAOLI, Via dei Tavolini 12r (between Via dei Cerchi and Via dei Calzaiuoli) – in the historic center. Monday, Wednesday – Sunday lunch and dinner. Phone: 055-216-215. *Moderate to Expensive.* A popular restaurant in a 16th - century palazzo in the historic Center (close to the Dante Museum). My delicious lunch was a huge antipasto (small samplings of cold cooked vegetables and seafood) followed by a plate of warm spring asparagus and for dessert, fresh berries topped with a liqueur. (Not bad for someone who normally swallows a tuna on pita in less than 10 minutes.)

RUTH'S KOSHER VEGETARIAN RESTAURANT, Via L.C. Farini 2r – next door to the synagogue. Phone: 055-248-0888. Hours: 12:30 – 2:30 pm and 8 – 10:30 pm, closed Friday evening and Saturday. *Inexpensive to Moderate.* A kosher restaurant that is a good spot for a light vegetarian lunch or dinner. Everything is freshly prepared.

**SOSTANZA, Via del Porcellana 25r –
down an alley-like street, close to S.
Trinite Church. Phone: 055-212-691.
No Credit Cards.** *Moderate.* A small
restaurant with delicious simple food at
reasonable prices. It is known for grilled
Florentine steaks and chicken breasts. I
met fun people at my crowded communal
table and loved my dinner.

**TRATTORIA ANTELLESI, Via Faenza
9r – near S. Lorenzo church and a
short walk from Palazzo Medici-
Riccardi. Phone: 055-216-990.**
Moderate. A small Italian trattoria owned
by an Italian-American couple. The pleasant ambience, friendly service and good
food make this a good choice for lunch
when sightseeing in the area.

**TRATTORIA IL TEATRO, Via degli
Alfani 47r – near Piazza Annunziata,
not far from Hotel Morandi Crocetta
or Monna Lisa. Phone: 055-247-9327.**
Moderate. A charming family-run trattoria.
I started with mussels lightly flavored with
garlic, lemon and white wine followed by
homemade pasta with a sauce of tomato
and fresh basil – simple and delicious. In
a lovely setting, it is highly recommended.

SOUTH SIDE

RISTORANTE LA GALLERIA, Via Guicciardini 48r–Oltrarno shopping district and Pitti Palace. Phone: 055-218-545. Closed Monday. *Moderate.* In this family restaurant, Rita is the chef and makes her own homemade pasta. Pino, her husband, will give you a warm welcome. A great lunch stop.

RISTORANTE PIEROT, Piazza Taddeo Gaddi 25r (Ponte alla Vittoria). Phone: 055-702-100. *Moderate.* On the south side of the Arno River–ten minute walk from hotels Ariele, Principe, Casa del Lago and Consigli–just cross the bridge, Ponte alla Vittoria, then cross the square to the far right side. You will enjoy a warm welcome from Gianni Martinoli followed by a dinner of fresh, scrumptious, Tuscan seafood. I love this friendly restaurant. Whether alone or with a group, you will be well received. Highly recommended.

TRATTORIA DEL CARMINE, Piazza del Carmine 18r. Phone: 055-218-601. Closed Sunday. *Moderate.* I ate the best antipasto salad and rabbit stew here in this small family trattoria. Great lunch spot if you are visiting the Brancacci Chapel at the Carmine Church.

LIGHT FARE AND DESSERTS

FRATELLINI, Via dei Cimatori 38r – Historic Center. Phone: 055-239-6096. Inexpensive. One of the oldest and last of minuscule outdoor standup wine bars in Florence. You can eat tiny crostini (open face sandwiches) or small panini (sandwiches) with a soft drink or glass of wine.

GILLI, Piazza della Repubblica 39r. Phone: 055-213-896. *Moderate.* Great people watching and a large selection of aperitifs, as well as great salads and desserts, make this historic café a popular stop. Enjoy a glass of wine at the bar where complimentary hors d'oeuvres are served in the early evening.

PROCACCI, Via Tornabuoni 64r. Phone: 055-211-656. *Moderate.* After a hard day of shopping a perfect late afternoon rest stop for a glass of wine or champagne and a couple of miniature sandwiches (salmon, vegetable, truffle, etc.).

There are a few small tables or you can stand at the tiny bar-counter. You can also purchase the gourmet products in attractive jars for great gifts.

RIVOIRE, Piazza della Signoria #5r. Phone: 055-214-412. Hours: Tuesday – Sunday, 8 am – Midnight. *Moderate.* Salads, sandwiches and the richest, sinful hot chocolate and cappuccino in town. They also sell wonderful assorted chocolates.

VIVOLI, Via Isola delle Stinche 7r – S. Croce District. Phone: 055-292-334. *Moderate.* Locals extol this as the best ice cream in the world. I loved it but still don't sneer at the other ice cream shops like Perché No. (Vivoli does not have cones because they claim the cone interferes with the purity of their ice cream.)

Whose bread and cheese I eat,
to his tune I dance.

- Florentine saying -

Mangiare Molto Bene
(To Eat Very Well)

A FEW POPULAR ITEMS

Antipasti – cooked room temperature
vegetables, marinated seafood,
spiced meats

Insalata verde – green salad

Insalata mista – mixed salad
(whatever they have – could be let-
tuce, carrots, tomatoes, fennel, etc.)

Insalata caprese – tomatoes, fresh
mozzarella cheese and basil (a spe-
cialty from the Isle of Capri – today
served everywhere)

Pizza Margherita – tomato, mozzarella and basil (originally made
in 17th- century Naples for Queen
Marguerite and now world known)

Risotto – rice cooked and flavored
with different vegetables or seafood

Carpaccio – paper thin slices of raw
beef, fish or smoked beef and served
often with parmesan cheese, arti-
chokes or mushrooms

Vitello tonnato – thin slices of room-temperature veal served with a sauce of tuna, olive oil, lemon and capers. A summertime favorite from Florence.

Ribollita - vegetable soup with beans and bread – a Florentine staple

Pasta papardelle – broad noodles with a sauce of tomato and rabbit (another Florentine staple)

Panini – sandwiches

Pesce spada – swordfish

Pesce locale – local fish

Paillard – a flat quickly cooked veal or chicken

Bistecca fiorentina – beef steak grilled, simply flavored with salt and pepper

Pollo – chicken

Vitello – veal

Contorini – cooked vegetables – spinaci (spinach), fagioli (beans), zucchini, melanzane (eggplant),

pepperoni (peppers, usu-
ally red peppers roasted),
funghi (mushrooms)

Legumi alla griglia –grilled vegetables

Crespelle – light pancakes with different stuffings like Mozzarella cheese

Crostini – toasted white bread with
toppings, such as tomato or truffle
paste.

Frutti di mare – seafood – sautéed
(mixed shellfish sautéed in olive oil),
vongole (clams), cozze (mussels)

Gnocchi – potato dumplings with
various fillings

Formaggio – cheese

Frutta – fruit

Gelato – ice cream

Té – tea

Caffé – coffee

Cappuccino – coffee with
steamed milk

San Pellegrino – Italian mineral
water - natural or effervescent

47

Florence is the
major cultural center
of Tuscany.

My Personal Favorites

MUSEUMS, CHURCHES, GALLERIES,
GARDENS & WALKS

When you have decided on your
Florentine travel dates, purchased air tickets and made hotel reservations, reserve
your museum tickets. Without reservations, the lines, particularly May through
October, are endless. Call one central
number for tickets for Uffizi, Accademia,
Medici Chapel and Pitti Palace (phone:
011-39-055-294-883). Try for early morning
(before 9:30 am), lunch time (12:45-1:15 pm)
or late in the day (after 4 pm). There is
also another group of museums owned by
the comune of Florence that sells a pass at
any city museum for 10,000 lire, which
entitles you to buy their ten member tickets at one-half off. Among them are the
Palazzo Vecchio and Brancacci Chapel.

> **Note:** Museum and church
> hours and fees change frequently
> in Italy. Confirm opening times
> and fees with your hotel or
> tourist office.

THE DUOMO, CAMPANILE and BAPTISTRY, Piazza del Duomo.
Hours: 8:30 am-6:20 pm Monday– Saturday, Sunday 1–5 pm. Phone: 055-230-2885. For thousands
of visitors, the starting point for the heart
of historic Florence is the Piazza del
Duomo – the square with three major pink,
green and white marble monuments
squeezed together: the Cathedral of S.
Maria del Fiore, called the Duomo, the
Baptistry and the Campanile. The
Cathedral of S. Maria del Fiore is among
the world's largest churches with
Westminster and St. Peter's a bit larger.
You can spot architect Brunelleschi's 15th-
century red tile dome from blocks away.
The enormous dome took 14 years to build
and is an architectural achievement, built
without scaffolds. (*Allow a minimum 45
minutes.*) Many of the original church
sculptures are across from the cathedral in
the Duomo Museum (Opera del Duomo).

THE MUSEO DEL OPERA DEL DUOMO (Duomo Museum), Piazza del Duomo 9. (The word opera here means works belonging to the Duomo not a museum of opera.) Hours: April-October, Monday – Saturday 9 am – 7:30 pm. November – March 9 am – 6:30 pm. Sundays 8:30 am – 2 pm. Phone: 055-230-2885. This small quiet museum has some major Renaissance sculptures that have been removed from their original settings for protection, such as Ghiberti's "Gates of Paradise" and Michelangelo's unfinished "Pietà." A few of my favorites are Donatello's "Magdalene," a powerful, rare gilded wood sculpture as well as the two cantorie (choir sculptures by Donatello and Luca della Robbia). *(Allow a minimum of 45 minutes.)*

CAMPANILE DEL DUOMO (Giotto's Belltower), Piazza del Duomo (2nd Bldg.) Hours: Open April–October, Daily 9 am – 6:50 pm. November – March, Daily 9 am – 5:30 pm. Phone: 055-230-2885. The Belltower (414 steps to the top) was designed and begun by Giotto and finished by Andrea

Pisano. If you have the energy and the line isn't too long, climb it for a picture-perfect view of Florence. (*Allow a few minutes if not climbing–one hour if going to the top.*)

BAPTISTRY – BATTISTERO DI S. GIOVANNI (3rd Bldg), (John the Baptist), Piazza del Duomo. Hours: Monday-Saturday, Noon – 6:30 pm. Sunday, 8:30 am – 1:30 pm. Phone: 055-230-2885. The Baptistry is known for its three gilded bronze doors by Andrea Pisano and Lorenzo Ghiberti. Ghiberti did the east and north doors; parts of the east door were damaged in the flood of 1966 and are now in the Duomo Museum. The east doors were nicknamed "Gates of Paradise" by Michelangelo. The octagonal baptistry is the oldest building in Florence, from the 11th- and 12th- centuries. The doors were added in the 14th- and 15th- centuries. (*Plan 1/2 hour to tour. It's the exterior that is most important here.*)

The Duomo complex is one of the busiest tourist spots in Florence. Pay attention to your valuables here or anywhere that you are in a crowd scene. Since this is the historic center of Florence, you will pass it many times on route to several historic and artistic venues.

GALLERIA DEGLI UFFIZI, Piazzale degli Uffizi. Hours: 8:30 am–6:50 pm, Daily except Mondays. Phone: 055-238-8651, Internet: <u>www.uffizi.com</u>. The Uffizi Gallery contains the world's most important collection of Italian Renaissance art. There are major works by all of the great Italian painters, as well as an extensive collection of Dutch and Flemish masterpieces. My personal favorites are the works of Duccio, Cimabue, Giotto and Botticelli's famous "Primavera" and "Birth of Venus." You should allow at least two hours for an overview. It is too much to absorb on any one visit. (*Last entrance is 30 minutes before closing.*)

MUSEO DEL BARGELLO, Via del Proconsolo, 4. Hours: Tuesday – Saturday 8:30 am – 1:50 pm, Sunday 9 am – 1 pm (confirm Sunday hours – they close certain Sundays). Phone: 055-238-8606. Like the Uffizi for major Renaissance paintings, this is the home for Renaissance sculptures with significant pieces by Donatello, Michelangelo and the Della Robbia family as well as many others. The building was a 13th-century fortress-like government building and hall of justice, later named for a police chief when it served as the city's jail. I love the outdoor staircase leading up from the inner courtyard filled with the coats of arms of the early justices. If it is not overly crowded, this is a wonderful place to enjoy the beautiful setting before ascending to the magnificent galleries on the 2^(nd) floor, including the collection of charming animal sculptures and Della Robbia's terracotta sculptures. (*Allow a minimum of 1 hours.*)

LOGGIA DELLA SIGNORIA, on the Piazza della Signoria. An outdoor sculpture gallery, which today has several copies, along with the recently restored "Perseus" by Cellini. On the square is a large copy of "David" by Michelangelo, along with Neptune's Fountain and a small disk that marks the spot where Savonarola was burned at the stake in 1498. On the side of the square and sculpture gallery is the Palazzo Vecchio–city hall and one time home of the Medici family. (*Allow 30 minutes.*)

CHURCH OF ORSANMICHELE, Via dei Calzaiuoli and Via dell'Arte della Lana. Hours: Monday–Friday 9–12 noon, 4–6 pm, Saturday 9 am–1 pm, 4–6 pm. Phone: 055-284-944. Originally built by the grain merchants' guild with a grain warehouse upstairs. Today you will find faded frescoes and stained glass in a dim, quiet interior on the ground floor. In the second floor museum are major sculptures

by Ghiberti, Donatello and Verrocchio,
that were once in the guild niches that
surround the exterior of the building.
(*Allow a minimum of 1 hour.*)

**CAPPELLE MEDICEE (Medici Chapels),
entrance on the side of S. Lorenzo
Church at the Piazza della Madonna d.
Aldobrandini. Hours: October-March
8:30 am-1:50 pm Tuesday-Saturday,
Sunday and some Mondays 8:30 am-
1:00 pm. April-September 8:30 am – 5 pm.
CHECK FIRST. Phone: 055-238-8602.**
Michelangelo designed these tombs for
the Medici family. My favorite is the "Night
and Day" sculpture in which he created
"Night" as a sleeping woman and "Day" as
a man awakening. Over four centuries ago
Michelangelo chiseled hard stone and today
we are still moved by his genius. MUST DO.
(*Allow a minimum of 45 minutes.*)

**BASILICA DI S. LORENZO, Piazza S.
Lorenzo. Hours: 7 am – 12 noon and
3:30-6:30 pm., Closed Sundays.
Phone: 055-216-634.**
Originally designed by Brunelleschi, this
lovely Renaissance church was commis-

sioned by the Medici Family in the 15th-
century. The interior was finished by
Michelangelo in the 16th- century. Watch
for Donatello's superb bronze relief
pulpits and the Old Sacristy created by
Brunelleschi along with the masterpieces
by Filippo Lippi and Verrocchio. On the
side is the Cloister that leads to the library
(Biblioteca Medicea-Laurenziana) with the
superb staircase designed by Michelangelo.
(*Allow a minimum of 45 minutes.*)

**GALLERIA DELL'ACCADEMIA, Via
Ricasoli, 60. Hours: Daily 8:30 am–
6:50 pm, Holidays. Closed Mondays.
Phone: 055-238-8609.** People come from
around the world to view Michelangelo's
powerful and beautiful "David." I have
never met anyone who was not overwhelmed by this incredible sculpture.
MUST DO. (*Allow a minimum of
45 minutes.*)

**MUSEO DI S. MARCO, Piazza S. Marco, 1.
Hours: Weekdays 8:30 am – 1:50 pm,
Saturday 8:30 am–6:50 pm. (Ticket
office closes 30 minutes before museum closing.) Open on some Sundays,
so call first. Phone: 055-238-8608.**
This lovely Dominican monastery was
built by Michelozzo. The multitude of
galleries on the first floor include the

Refettorio (dining hall) with a "Last Supper" by Ghirlandaio and a beautiful cloister. The "Annunciation" plus the exquisite frescoes painted by Fra Angelico and his students are located on the second floor in the individual cells of the monks. I had a lunch date and felt anxiety ridden because I could not linger and enjoy this quiet, elegant museum with its countless masterpieces. For art lovers a **MUST DO!** (Be sure to *allow at least 1 ½ hours here.*)

S. CROCE CHURCH and MONASTERY, Piazza S. Croce. Hours: Summer 9:30 am–5:30 pm, Winter 8 am–12:30 pm and 3 pm–5:30 pm, Sundays 3–5:30 pm. Phone: 055-244-619. In Florence you can become jaded by so many magnificent churches filled with masterpiece paintings and sculptures. But please save some energy for this famous Florentine church with its amazing collection of fine art. It is also the final resting place of many Italian notables, including Michelangelo. I love the Giotto frescoes in the Bardi and Peruzzi Chapels and the elegant Pazzi Chapel begun by architect Brunelleschi with terracotta apostles by Luca della Robbia. Take a good guidebook or an art tour here. There is so much to see. (*Allow a minimum of 1 hour.*)

LA SINAGOGA DI FIRENZE, Via Farini 4/6. Hours: Sunday–Thursday 10 am–1 pm and 2–5 pm. Phone: 055-234-6654. This unusual synagogue and museum were built in the mid-19th- century in the style of Hagia Sophia, the famous Byzantine church in Istanbul. Upstairs is a small museum of Jewish ceremonial objects and photographs of the old ghetto. (*Allow 45 minutes for the tour.*)

MUSEO HORNE, Via de' Benci #6 (at the end of Borgo S. Croce). Hours: Monday–Saturday 9 am–1 pm, Closed Sundays and Holidays. Phone: 055-244-661. An Englishman's private collection of 14th - 16th - century art and artifacts like the ancient eating utensils as well as the art collection in this fascinating Renaissance palace. (*Allow a minimum of 1 hour.*)

S. MARIA NOVELLA CHURCH and CLOISTERS (next to the train station) Hours: 9:30 am–5 pm, Friday and Sunday 1–5 pm. Phone: 055-210-113. This enormous church with its Gothic interior has many individual chapels filled with Renaissance masterpieces. Take time to see the Cappella Strozzi at the left end of the transept. Also see works by Masaccio, Brunelleschi and Giotto, to name a few. (*Allow a minimum of 1 hour.*)

**BRANCACCI CHAPEL in the Church
of S. Maria del Carmine, Piazza del
Carmine. Hours: 10 am – 5 pm. Sunday
1–5 pm, Closed Tuesdays. Phone: 055-
238-2195.** This intimate chapel was built
by the Brancacci family in the 15th-century.
They commissioned the leading realist
painter, Masaccio, along with Masolino,
to paint the awe-inspiring frescoes that
were completed by Filippino Lippi 50
years later. The entire chapel is an out-
standing example of Renaissance painting
not to be missed.

(*Allow a minimum of 40 minutes.*)

**S. SPIRITO CHURCH, Piazza S. Spirito.
Hours: 8 am–12 noon, 4–6 pm, closed
Wednesday. Phone: 055-210-030.**
A 15th-century church started by architect
Brunelleschi and finished after his death.
The church has recently acquired a mag-
nificent small crucifix by Michelangelo.
The beautiful gray and white interior
will remind you of the Piazza Annunziata.
The church is on the side of the charming
square S. Spirito, where there are some
cafés and a Tuesday street market.

(*Allow a minimum of 45 minutes.*)

PITTI PALACE and BOBOLI GARDENS (2 separate tickets). Hours: Palatine Gallery (main art gallery of Pitti Palace): 8:30 am – 6:50 pm, Closed Mondays. Boboli Gardens: Winter 9 am – 4:30 pm, Spring, Summer and Fall 9 am – 6 pm. Phone: 055-238-8614. Built from the 15th- to the 18th- century, this was where the Medici family moved after living in the Palazzo Vecchio. In the elegant galleries you will see major works by Titian, Rubens, Raphael, Caravaggio and Andrea del Sarto, as well as others, collected through the centuries by the Medici family. The palace overlooks the enormous park-like Boboli Gardens, which makes a great relaxing stop after your palace tour. In the gardens, you are in the countryside in the middle of Florence. The grounds go on for acres, filled with formal greenery, statuary, fountains, lakes and panoramic views. It is another wonderful spot to indulge your imagination and pretend you are a Florentine princess out for a stroll. (*Allow a minimum of 2 1/2 hours.*)

CHIESA DI S. MINIATO AL MONTE (Church of S. Miniato al Monte), Viale Galileo. Hours: Open Daily. 8 am–12 noon and 2:30–6 pm. Phone: 055-234-2731. A 10-minute bus ride to Piazzale Michelangelo, then a 5-minute walk uphill (take Bus #12 or #13 at Ponte alla Grazie – on the south side – one bridge east of Ponte Vecchio) or walk up the steps (behind Silla Hotel) in Via S. Niccolò. This 11th-to 13th-century Romanesque church on top of a high hill in Florence is spectacular. I love the setting above the Piazzale Michelangelo with the stunning view of the Tuscan hills and Florence spread beneath you. The façade and simple interior includes the softly faded frescoes and terra cotta ceiling by Luca della Robbia. Hopefully you will be able to time your visit for when the monks sing vespers in Gregorian chant. (*Check times with concierge and allow a minimum of 2 hours.*)

FAVORITE WALKS, GARDENS and VIEWS

- Walk anywhere along the Arno River, particularly at sunrise or dusk.

- Spend a quiet moment or breakfast in a private garden like the gardens of hotels Ariele, Principe, Monna Lisa or Hotel Classic.

- Walk down to Villa S. Michele or Bencistà Pensione from Fiesole.

- Enjoy the view from the Etruscan Ruins in Fiesole.

- Walks in the Tuscan Hills with the gorgeous views of Florence from Forte Belvedere, Torre Bellesguardo, or the stairway up to S. Miniato.

- Spend a few minutes in any of the lovely cloistered church gardens, such as the Carmine, S. Lorenzo and S. Marco, or in the courtyard of the Bargello Museum.

- Enjoy the terrace outside S. Miniato Church overlooking all of Florence for a spectacular vista and a moment of reflection.

- Stroll the Boboli Gardens with its beautiful views and wonderful quiet spots to just sit and relax.

Shopping

HIGHLIGHTS
AND OFF-THE-BEATEN-TRACK

NORTH SIDE OF ARNO RIVER

In the historic north side of Florence, the streets are filled with well-known designer stores, particularly Via Calzaiuoli, Via Tornabuoni, Via Por S. Maria and Via Strozzi. Window-shopping after dinner is a popular Italian pastime. (**Don't forget this tip for finding addresses:** commercial address has a **lowercase "r"** after street number; residential address, an **uppercase "R"**)

Ferragamo, Via Tornabuoni 14r. Phone: 055-292-123. On one of the main shopping streets, Via Tornabuoni, is the palace which today houses the gorgeous Ferragamo store (men's and women's elegant ready-to-wear as well as an excellent shoe and accessory department). While the dollar is high, shoes and handbags are a great bargain. Upstairs you can visit the shoe museum filled with Hollywood memorabilia–by appointment only (phone 055-336-0456). I found it fascinating, particularly the photos of Audrey Hepburn and Marilyn Monroe wearing Ferragamo shoes and the displays of elegant footwear.

For Gold Jewelry, Tourist Trinkets and Toys – The Ponte Vecchio

The old bridge that connects the north and south bank of the Arno River is jammed with tourists buying similar expensive gold jewelry and trinkets from dozens of gold-smiths and artisans. (Check out Melli for antique jewelry.) The joys of great bargains are long gone, so shop carefully before you buy. For many women, this is the highlight of their Florentine trip; for others it is too commercial, too crowded and a place to avoid. Whatever your personal feeling, don't miss at least a look at this historic bridge with its colorful history. Originally, the shops all belonged to butchers and tanners until Cosimo I had Vasari build the corridor to connect the Palazzo Vecchio and the Uffizi to his new home, the Pitti Palace, on the south side. He disliked the smells and blood and invited the more upscale local goldsmiths, jewelers and silversmiths to move into some 40 shops. Watch your own valuables here because pickpockets prey on American tourists.

Shopping for Leather

The leather school at S. Croce Church and all the shops around S. Croce as well as the markets and every major shopping street on both sides of the Arno River. Don't hesitate to shop unfamiliar names. Many small Italian manufacturers do not export but have excellent quality.

For inexpensive basic sweaters, Florentine paper, toys, handbags, leathers, fashion accessories and scarves (best buys – paper products and accessories):

- **S. Lorenzo Market –** All around and behind the Central Market and the S. Lorenzo Church.

- **Straw Market –** Much smaller than S. Lorenzo Market, the Straw Market is also called Mercato Nuovo and Porcellino. It is located between the Piazza della Repubblica and Ponte Vecchio on Via Por S. Maria.

At both markets, check out the synthetic Pashmina shawls in dozens of colors. They feel and look like cashmere and sell for under $25.

Coin, Via Calzaiuoli 56r. Phone: 055-280-531.

A small department store centrally located near the Duomo that offers tax free shopping, moderate priced fashions and a good selection of accessories, handbags, scarves and housewares. BEST OF ALL, THEY HAVE A POWDER ROOM ON THE TOP FLOOR. (Finding decent toilets in Italy is always a challenge.)

**After Dark, Via de'Ginori 47r.
Phone: 055-294-203.**
This is an English language bookstore –
great for novels, guides and Tuscan history
or art books.

**Passamaneria Toscana, Piazza S.
Lorenzo 12r. Phone: 055-214-670.**
Large selection of handmade stunning
tassels, tie backs, tapestries, etc. (The
tassels make great gifts. They are used all
over Europe as drawer pulls.) This is the
main store and it is located near the
Medici Chapel at S. Lorenzo. The prices
are much less than in the States.

**Loretta Caponi, Piazza Antinori 4r.
Phone: 055-213-668.**
Handmade table and bed linens, gorgeous
lingerie, baby clothes and real "hankies."
Super extravagant, elegant merchandise in
a museum-like historic building complete
with frescoed ceilings. Buy a few handker-
chiefs for gifts. The wrapping is terrific. If
you want to feel like Italian aristocracy,
don't miss this store.

**Pineider, Piazza della Signoria 13r.
Phone: 055-284-655.**
For elegant stationery, visit this
superb store.

Furla, Via Calzaiuoli 47r.
Phone: 055-238-2883.
Expensive status handbags popular with
American women. The prices are currently
cheaper in Italy than in New York.

Profumeria Inglese, Via Tornabuoni 97r.
Phone: 055-289-7548.
For make-up, cosmetics and perfumes. A
centrally located store if you need a new
lipstick, eyeliner, etc (not cheap). Staff
speaks English and I found them helpful.

Hito, Via de'Ginori 21r.
Phone: 055-284-424.
Complete beauty treatments, massage,
facials, manicures and pedicures in a
small elegant historic setting complete
with a frescoed ceiling and back courtyard garden. Open by appointment
from Monday to Saturday. (Not far from
Duomo and S. Lorenzo Market, this makes
a great relaxing break from sightseeing
and shopping.)

Alessandra Bizzari, Via Condotta 32r.
Phone: 055-211-580.
A charming old chemist shop right in the
center of historic Florence. You can buy
small packages of herbs and spices as well
as a variety of face creams and lotions.
There are no samples to try so you buy on
faith but the experience of shopping here
is like being transported in time. You will
love the antique fittings of this old apothe-
cary shop.

A Do-Not-Miss Florentine Experience:
Officina Profumo – Farmacia di S.
Maria Novella, Via della Scala 16r.
Phone: 055-216-276.
This is one of the world's oldest pharma-
cies. The Dominican fathers started grow-
ing herbs in their adjacent garden for
medicinal purposes in the 1300s. In the
16th- century, they expanded their products
to perfumes and cosmetics. In the 19th-
century, a private family bought the pharmacy and continued to add new items.
Today their products are still sold in the
same magnificent late medieval building
as well as globally. They have an extensive
list of perfumes, herbal remedies, cosmetics, soaps and potpourri in a setting fit for
a queen's coronation or a royal wedding.
Even if you do not buy anything, pretend
you are a Medici princess ordering your
beauty supplies.

Filatura Di Crosa, Via Guicciardini 21r: A yarn shop for unusual yarns at great prices.

For the inexhaustible shopper:
A few other fashion streets: Via Porta Rossa, Via della Condotta, Via del Corso, Via Ghibellina, plus all the street merchants and shops on the quay along the north bank of the Arno River.

SOUTH SIDE OF ARNO RIVER – OLTRARNO DISTRICT

On the south side of the Arno River you will find delightful artisan shops that sell jewelry, handbags, gloves, silver, antiques and arts and crafts. The main shopping streets here are: Borgo S. Jacopo, Via S. Spirito, Borgo S. Frediano, Via Maggio, Via Romana, Via Guicciardini. Here are a few suggestions:

**Antico Setificio Fiorentino, Via
Bartolini 4r. Phone: 055-213-861.
Hours: Monday – Friday 9 am – 1pm,
2 pm – 5 pm.**

An antique weaving studio from 1686,
purchased by Emilio Pucci before his
death. Today it is run by one of his associ-
ates and features some of the most elegant
hand-woven decorator fabrics and pillows
as well as beautiful affordable boutique
gifts (miniature address books, picture
frames, jewelry, pouches, etc.) exquisitely
gift wrapped. You ring the courtyard bell
and enter through a historic garden. The
weavers are in the building on the left.
Ask to see them at work. On the right is
the showroom where you make your
selections. Like the Farmacia di
S. Maria Novella, this is a unique
Florentine shopping experience.

**Giulio Giannini & Figlio, Piazza Pitti 37r.
Phone: 055-212-621.**

Expensive, marbleized Florentine paper
goods popular with Florentines as well
as tourists. The note paper makes
gorgeous gifts.

**Madova, Via Guicciardini – 1r.
Phone: 055-239-6526.**

Gloves from $18 up. They have a huge
selection of colors and styles in this
minute store.

**Acqua Fortis, Borgo S. Jacopo 80r.
Phone: 055-292-164.**
Antique flower pictures. Tiny shop
crammed with stocks of flower pictures
from $15 up.

**Paolo Pagliai, Borgo S. Jacopo 41r.
Phone: 055-282-840.** Silversmith
A small shop filled with antique silver
pieces as well as reproductions.

Roberta, Borgo S. Jacopo 74–78r.
Gloves, scarves and handbags. Moderately
priced gloves from $18 up but not as large
a selection as Madova.

On Borgo S. Frediano. Dozens of small
jewelry shops. Contemporary, antique,
semi-precious and costume. Prices are
moderate to expensive.

**Punt Oro, Via S. Spirito 11r.
Phone: 055-289-327.**
Expensive fine jewelry. This is like visiting a small contemporary Tiffany showroom. They do beautiful custom jewelry.
You can buy a small gold chain bracelet
for under $100 or a fabulous ring for a

few thousand. If you are in the market for
real jewelry, do check out Punt Oro. It is
inside No. 11, halfway down the corridor
on the right-hand side. If you pass it, the
corridor ends at a charming garden which
belongs to S. Spirito Church. Take a minute
to enjoy this hidden treasure.

Geraldine Tayar, Sdrucciolo dei Pitti 6r. Phone: 055-290-405.

A wonderful boutique of ready-to-wear,
accessories and hats designed by a talented
Florentine. This is definitely off-the-beaten-path. I found it on route to the Pitti
Palace from S. Spirito Church. The fashions here do not look like standard
department store merchandise.

Ponte Vecchio, Borgo S. Jacopo 38r. Phone: 055-215-654.

Nice purses, be sure to ask what is their
best-discounted price. The owners, the
Osti family, speak excellent English and
are anxious to do business.

Marionette da Salotto, Via Romana 89r. Phone: 055-299-272.

Puppets. I discovered this lovely shop
filled with handmade puppets, both
antique and contemporary, walking to the
Romana Gate from the Pitti Palace. Each
puppet was fascinating. There are charac-
ters out of Italian operas and mythological

creatures. From $25 up, up, up, you can buy a small child's puppet or a true collector's item.

A few favorite places of very hard-shopping American friends, along with their comments:

Freon, Via Guicciardini 118r:
"Cool, hip stuff."

Gioielleria Piccini Ugo e Figlio, Via Por S. Maria 9/11r: *"Fine jewelry at fair prices."* This is also listed in every guidebook.

These are a few shopping treasures. For a more complete list, check *"Born to Shop – Italy"* by Suzy Gershman, published by Frommer's.

Follow Lynn through narrow
medieval streets where
she'll lead you to the greatest
Renaissance treasures
as well as 21st-century dining
and shopping.

How to See Florence
Suggested Itineraries

*To fully experience the richness of
Florence, you should try to plan at least
five full days. If your time is limited,
however, these are a few suggestions that
can be covered in two days:*

TWO-DAY ITINERARY:
DAY ONE

➢ Take a Walking Tour.

➢ Accademia to see "David," walking
past Brunelleschi's Piazza SS.
Annunziata.

➢ In S. Lorenzo Church visit the Medici
Chapel and the library and staircase
by Michelangelo.

➢ Shop S. Lorenzo Market.

➢ Shop Farmacia di S. Maria Novella for
great cosmetics and perfumes made
from 16th - century recipes.

➢ Shop Via Tornabuoni – the elegant
street of designer boutiques.

➢ Stop for a drink (Procacci or
Cantinetta Antinori).

DAY TWO

➢ Ferragamo Shoe Museum and Store.

➢ Shop Antico Setificio for gifts out of
  remnants of hand-loomed fabrics

➢ Brancacci Chapel to see Masaccio,
  Masolino and Filippino Lippi's
  frescoes.

➢ Shop Oltrarno District for crafts,
  jewelry, leathers, etc.

➢ Pitti Palace and Boboli Gardens to
  see how the Medicis lived.

➢ S. Miniato Church with views of
  Florence.

➢ Uffizi Gallery to see the greatest
  collection of Renaissance art.

➢ Gilli or Rivoire for a drink.

FIVE-DAY ITINERARY
DAY ONE:
A WALK AROUND ORIENTATION

Here is a suggested itinerary for five days. Select from it according to your own personal interests and energy and enjoy Florence at your own pace!

➤ After an early morning international arrival in Rome or Milan, you will either connect with a short flight to Florence or transfer to the train station, arriving between 10 am and noon. If your room is not ready, you can freshen up in the powder room and go out for a leisurely walk and overview.

➤ **A few suggestions to acquaint you with Florence:** Before leaving your hotel, pick up the map and have the concierge show you exactly where you are and the location of the Ponte Vecchio, the Uffizi, Piazza della Repubblica and the Duomo, as well as north and south orientation.

➤ Walk over to the Ponte Vecchio, the historic bridge spanning the Arno River. You will see jewelers and tourist stands of all kinds. Besides the fabulous view of Florence from the middle of the bridge, you will get an idea of the current Florentine merchandise you will be seeing or buying on the rest of your visit. The area is filled with tourists and pickpockets, so pay attention!

➤ At the north side of the bridge, turn right and walk to the world-famous Florentine gallery, the Uffizi. Turn left, passing the whole length of the gallery until you arrive at the Palazzo Vecchio, the old palace with the copy of Michelangelo's "David" standing outside. Turn left here. You are now standing in the Piazza della Signoria with its outdoor sculpture gallery. Next walk over to the Via Calzaiuoli and turn right. At Via del Corso, turn left arriving at the large square, Piazza della Repubblica.

➤ Stop for a light lunch at Gilli, a famous old café, and enjoy this typical Florentine scene. (Table service is double that of ordering at the bar.) To continue your stroll, walk back to Via Calzaiuoli and turn left. Keep going until you run into the Piazza del Duomo.

➤ The Duomo complex is the center of historic Florence. Here you will find three major Renaissance architectural masterpieces: the Cathedral of S. Maria del Fiore called the Duomo, Giotto's Belltower, and the Baptistry. Walk around the interior of this huge cathedral. (You will return tomorrow with your walking tour for a more detailed visit.)

➤ Stroll back to your hotel. Be sure you have your hotel card as well as your map with you so people can point you in the right direction. Florentines are incredibly gracious and patient, giving thousands of lost tourists constant directions, so don't hesitate to ask. (I get lost on every trip!) Ask the concierge to make dinner reservations at a nearby restaurant for 9 pm.

➤ Unpack and sleep for a few hours before going to dinner. Dress in a pant or skirt outfit with your small purse and jewelry. The Florentines are rather conservative and elegant in their dress at a good restaurant and much more casual at a trattoria or pizzeria.

➤ Enjoy your first dinner of simple but
   delicious Tuscan cooking and after dinner, do as the Italians do – walk off your
   dinner by window-shopping and stop
   for a teensy gelato (ice cream) that is
   worth every calorie. Continue back to
   your hotel and don't be embarrassed
   if you have to ask directions again.
   **Always have your map and hotel
   card with you.**

SLEEP WELL! (*Buon riposo!*)

DAY TWO
YOUR FIRST DAY OF SIGHTSEEING

➤ Get an early start so you can enjoy
   your buffet breakfast at a leisurely pace
   or read the monthly tourist magazine
   called *Concierge*, available free in the
   hotels or at the tourist bureau. It lists
   current happenings, concerts, etc., as
   well as current hours for museums and
   churches. Before leaving, ask the
   concierge to make dinner reservations.
   (A few of my favorites are Pierot for
   seafood, Sostanza for grilled meat and

chicken and i'Parione for superb pasta and other Tuscan specialties.) Also have the concierge show you on your map exactly where the meeting place is for the walking tour of Florence.

➤ Follow your guide and learn a bit of Renaissance history, art, gossip and folklore to enhance your enjoyment of this fascinating artistic city. Since central Florence no longer allows cars, walking tours are the way to go. I recommend "The Original and Best Walking Tour of Florence." They divide you into small groups of four to eight people and the cost is under $20 (055-2645033).

When the tour ends, ask the guide for directions to a nearby bar to have a quick salad or sandwich, and to show you on the map exactly where you are.

➤ Find your way back to the Uffizi gallery where you have pre-reserved your ticket so you can avoid the long lines. Take a small guidebook to help identify the important works of art (see Resources).

If you want more detailed information on Renaissance art, you can also take a tour with an art historian. (The walk-

ing tour companies as well as hotel
concierge or your travel agent can
make the arrangements.) Rates vary
from about $35 to $100.

➤ Take a refreshment break on the terrace
at the Uffizi. This gallery needs several
visits and hopefully you will return
many times.

➤ Walk over to the Accademia to see
"David." Follow signs back to the
Duomo – then on the far side of the
Duomo, follow Via Ricasoli to Galleria
dell' Accademia.

➤ After entering the museum (with your
reserved ticket) and after viewing the
wonderful massive unfinished sculptures by Michelangelo, you will sudden-
ly be in front of "David." Look at it –
walk around it and savor it again.

➤ Leave the museum and walk around
the block to Piazza SS. Annunziata,
the lovely square designed in part by
Brunelleschi. On the Square are the
historic church and the foundling
hospital where unwanted babies were
left during the Renaissance. There
are beautiful blue and white circular
sculptures (called tondos) of infants by
Della Robbia on the exterior walls in
glazed terracotta.

➤ Across the square is a Renaissance building that today houses the lovely Hotel
Loggiato dei Serviti. Unfortunately, in
the evening this square also serves as
the meeting and sleeping place for
young international drifters.

➤ Continue back to the Duomo on Via
dei Servi – about two blocks from the
Piazza. If you want to shop, follow
the signs to Ponte Vecchio (walking on
Via Calzaiuoli which is one of the main
north-south streets) or any side street
that looks interesting. The other
choice is just to relax at a café or
visit the department store Coin on Via
Calzaiuoli, starting at the ladies room
on the top floor and working your way
down to the main floor for reasonable,
fun accessories.

➤ Return to your hotel and rest.

➢ At dinner, be adventurous by trying one new dish! With all of the walking, you can enjoy a few extra treats without fear of gaining weight.

➢ After dinner, window shop or stop at an outside café for coffee and people watching (another important Italian pastime).

➢ Sleep well – *you should be exhausted!*

DAY THREE

➢ First stop, the Cappelle Medicee. (Medici Chapels)

➢ From the Ponte Vecchio, walk straight up Via Por S. Maria which changes names to Via Calimala, then to Via Roma. Cross the Duomo Piazza with the Baptistry on your right and continue straight. The street is now called Borgo S. Lorenzo. Turn left at Via del Canto de' Nelli. Walk around S. Lorenzo Church to the Cappelle Medicee entrance.

➢ Visit this elegant jewel and be prepared to be overwhelmed when you see the Medici tombs sculpted by Michelangelo.

➤ Walk around to the entrance for the church and library with Michelangelo's staircase. Pay your fee (this is new) and visit the church. Refer to your guidebook to find the major works of art.

➤ Walk over to S. Maria Novella Church, which is towards the train station. (This is another church that now charges a fee.) I personally love this church with its façade of green and white marble. The church is a veritable Renaissance museum. Keep your guidebook open and visit the different chapels built for individual wealthy families.

➤ Exit the church and bear right. Walk past the Minerva Hotel (once a Dominican convent) and at the street Via Scala turn right. Walk a few blocks until you come to the historic Farmacia di S. Maria Novella, Via Scala #16.

➤ Farmacia di S. Maria Novella is one of Florence's true treasures. A monastery founded in the 13th-century where you can buy beauty products, herbal cures and perfumes made from the ancient recipes of the Dominican friars. The palatial building has frescoed ceilings, elegant woodwork and cloistered gardens. This is my idea of great gift

shopping. Don't forget to pick up a copy
of the product list so you can re-order
by e-mail. They ship worldwide.
Shopping here is delightful!

➤ Walk back to S. Lorenzo Church and
market. On the far side of the market
turn left for the Central Food Market –
it's the pinkish building. Go into this
huge covered food market with gorgeous displays of flowers, fruits,
vegetables, poultry, meats, cheeses,
etc. Find Nerbone, a small café that is a
Florentine tradition in the corner of the
first floor. Have a coffee or lunch here
while watching 21st-century Florentines
going about their daily lives. The other
choice is to save lunch for a trattoria
near the church, like Trattoria Antellesi
(see Restaurants) or the chic Cantinetta
Antinori (*a ten-minute walk*).

➤ Shop S. Lorenzo Market all around the
church or have a long leisurely lunch.
If shopping S. Lorenzo's outdoor market
a word of caution: Think, is the merchandise really different from home,
cheaper, as good quality, something you
will really use or just adding pounds to
your luggage? If you love something,
buy it; but if you are lukewarm, forget
it. You can never return it!

➤ Walk back to the Duomo (follow signs –
Borgo S. Lorenzo takes you back to
the Duomo complex). At the rear of the
cathedral, cross the street to the Museo
dell' Opera del Duomo. Here you can
see up close the fabulous original
art removed from the Duomo and
Baptistry for safekeeping.

➤ Walk over to Ferragamo Shoe Museum
and store which is on the corner of
Via Tornabuoni and the quay of the
Arno. Go to the entrance address #2
Tornabuoni. Your concierge can make
a reservation for a free visit to the
Ferragamo Shoe Museum (055-336-0456)
Via Tornabuoni 2 (usually Monday,
Wednesday and Friday 9am–1pm and
2–6pm but also subject to change). The
museum is on the third floor of a magnificent 14th-century Florentine palace
which today houses the world headquarters as well as the huge store with
designer shoes, accessories and ready-
to-wear on the first floor. The museum
is fun and a welcome change from all
of the religious Renaissance art that
you have been absorbing.

➤ Walk down Via Tornabuoni, shopping all of the designer stores. Be sure to visit Laura Caponi (lingerie, linens and baby clothes – all handmade) in a luxurious historic palace with frescoed ceiling. Stop like a Florentine resident for a glass of Prosecco (Italian sparkling wine) and a tiny open faced sandwich at Proccaci (see Restaurants).

➤ Return to your hotel and change for an evening concert, opera or ballet. Enjoy the performance and then have a late, light supper or sinful dessert before returning to your hotel for a good night's rest.

DAY FOUR

➤ **Antico Setificio Fiorentino, Via Bartolini 4 (week days only)**. Cross the Arno River at Ponte A. Vespucci to visit the south side of Florence. Start in the Oltrarno District, the shopping area of assorted artisans, crafts, art galleries, jewelers, antique dealers, leather shops and unusual boutiques. After crossing the bridge continue straight for one block until Via Bartolini. Turn right and walk down to #4 on the right (north side) of the street. Ring the bell and you

will be greeted and brought through the historic courtyard and garden of this ancient weaving studio into the elegant showroom. This is another unique Florentine experience. In the showroom are fabulous expensive hand-loomed decorator fabrics and pillows, but in an alcove there are small charming picture frames, address books, large or tiny photo albums, pin cushions, etc; perfect small gifts from $10 up that they will gift wrap in little bags with their seal. These chic accessories are made from remnants of the gorgeous hand-loomed fabrics. Before you leave, ask directions for the Carmine Church (*five minute walk*).

➤ At the Carmine Church, visit the splendid Brancacci chapel with the beautiful frescoes by Masaccio, Masolino and Filippino Lippi. This is one of my personal favorites.

➤ Walk toward the Pitti Palace (there are signs directing you) window shopping or stopping along the way. A few streets with interesting shopping are Borgo S. Frediano, Via S. Spirito, Via Mazzetta and Borgo S. Jacopo. Make your own shopping discoveries.

91

➤ Stop and have a quick sandwich or salad before your visit to Pitti Palace, either at a bar or the restaurant in the Pitti Palace.

➤ Tour the luxurious Pitti Palace, former home of the Medici family, with their enormous art collection in the galleries. (This is another museum where you should pre-order tickets.)

➤ Right behind the Pitti Palace are the world famous Boboli Gardens. Walk through a small section or sit on a park bench and enjoy the local children at play. This is a great spot just to relax.

➤ Exit Pitti Palace and either hoof it or take Bus #13 from Ponte alle Grazie up to Piazzale Michelangelo, the square with the views overlooking Florence. Stop at the café, rest and enjoy this spectacular panorama. Next, walk up the hill for about five minutes until you reach S. Miniato and its terrace, with an even more fantastic view of Florence and the surrounding hills.

➤ Hopefully you have arrived in time at this gem of a Romanesque church for the early evening Gregorian chants. The architecture, façade, paintings and setting all will contribute to making this a high point of your trip. It is another of my favorite places in Florence. (Check for the exact time for the chants. They vary.)

➤ Take the bus back to Ponte alle Grazie or walk down the stairs. (Watch for the miniature "Cat Houses" on your left hand side. This is the cat sanctuary of Florence.)

➤ Find a little café facing the Arno or have high tea at a glamorous hotel such as the Helvetia e Bristol, Grand Hotel or Excelsior.

➤ Tonight enjoy another performance followed by a light supper.

DAY FIVE

➤ "Buongiorno, prima colazione per favore" (good morning, breakfast please). By now you are probably fluent in tourist Italian.

➤ Walk over to the Bargello Museum on Via del Proconsolo. The Bargello is not overwhelming in size like the Uffizi. The former historic town hall, hall of justice and police headquarters is an interesting setting for this fabulous sculpture collection.

➤ Turn right when you exit the Bargello Museum onto Via del Proconsolo and walk until you come to Via dei Servi – the small street across from the Duomo

on the right hand side. Turn right and
walk a few blocks to the Piazza della SS.
Annunziata. Cross the Piazza and turn
left onto Via C. Battista. Just up the
street on the right hand side you will
see the Museo di S. Marco, one of the
loveliest museums in Florence. The Fra
Angelico frescoes are compelling.

➤ On S. Marco Square, take Bus #7 to
Fiesole. (Have your concierge confirm
the bus number. Several buses stop at
the same sign so be sure you get on the
right one for Fiesole.) It is only a 20-
minute trip and the buses run every
20 minutes.

➤ Fiesole, the ancient hill town overlooking
Florence, is filled with Etruscan ruins,
small museums and views that don't
stop. Start with lunch at the trattoria on
the main square; then decide whether
you want to walk in the hills, visit the
Etruscan ruins, the Roman amphitheater,
the museums or cathedral.

➤ An interesting walk (about 15 minutes)
is down the road to Villa S. Michele, a
15th- century monastery that today is
a 40-room super elegant luxury hotel.
You could have a drink or call ahead for
lunch reservations (055-59451) or walk
a little farther downhill to visit the
Pensione Bencistà, a 13th- century

monastery that today is an inexpensive 44-room pensione with incredible views and gardens.

➤ Take the bus back to Piazza S. Marco.

➤ If you enjoy a long walk, after returning to Piazza S. Marco on the bus, follow your map to S. Croce or take the tourist bus C. Visit this important church brimming with great art and tombs of many Italian notables. Leave the main church at the far right side and visit the leather factory, which is a school started by the Franciscan monks at the end of World War II to give employment to poor Florentine youths. Today it is a flourishing business selling leather goods to international tourists. It is the only church I know where you can shop for handbags, wallets, card cases, etc., then return to the chapel to pray. In the first cloister (separate entrance) is the Museo dell' Opera di S. Croce. Inside you first come upon the Cappella Pazzi. This exquisite quiet chapel, designed by Brunelleschi (also the architect of S. Lorenzo and the cathedral dome) with the beautiful Della Robbia ceramics and massive carved doors by da Maiano is a wonderful spot to rest and reflect.

➤ Find a café in either the S. Croce district or walk or take the tourist bus to Piazza della Signoria or Repubblica and revive with a drink or coffee while watching the colorful street scene.

➤ Return to your hotel, soak in the tub, put your feet up and write postcards or jot down some of the wonderful experiences in your travel diary and even the dreadful faux pas that later will become wonderful comical memories. I still enjoy all the unexpected experiences that happen to me on every trip.

➤ Go out for a delicious dinner, which you have reserved in advance, relax and enjoy every bite.

Pleasant dreams!

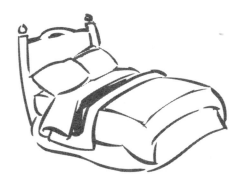

For More-Timers or Many-Timers

➢ Dante Museum (055-219-416) – a small museum with artifacts of Dante's life and works – I personally loved this building in the historic center, Via S. Margherita 1.

➢ Palazzo Medici – Riccardi, Via Camillo Cavour 3r (055-276-0340) – home of Cosimo and Lorenzo de' Medici, with spectacular 15th-century frescoes by Gozzoli–not far from the Duomo and S. Lorenzo.

➢ Palazzo Vecchio with the Medici Apartments, particularly Eleanor of Toledo's rooms, Piazza della Signoria (055-276-8465).

➢ Museo Archeologico, Via della Colonna 38r (055-23575).

➢ Botanical Gardens, near Piazza S. Marco.

➢ Casa Buonarroti, Via Ghibellina #70 (055-241-752) – a small museum of Michelangelo built by his nephew.

➢ Walks along the north or south shore of the Arno River.

➤ Walks up in the hills to Forte del Belvedere or Torre Bellosguardo.

➤ Walk up the steps to S. Miniato. Be sure to notice on the right-hand side half way up the miniature domiciles for stray cats. This feline sanctuary was started by a cat-loving woman and now the local residents continue to bring food and water to this unusual "cat house." The official sign reads: "Colonia Felina – Protetia." Across from the cat colony on the left-hand side is a rose garden – open daily 8:30 am – 12:30 pm.

➤ Bicycle or walking tour of Tuscany.

➤ A leisurely return to any of your favorite places.

➤ Visit Chianti wineries and local markets – take a cooking lesson.

➤ Day trips either on your own or with a tour to Siena and other Tuscan hill towns.

On Your Own to Siena
One of the Jewels of Tuscany

A SAMPLE ITINERARY
FOR A DAY TRIP

Siena is so close to Florence and such an easy pleasurable journey that I highly recommend at least one day in this gorgeous medieval city.

The bus ride is less than a 1½ hour trip through the Tuscan countryside with ancient vineyards and olive farms. This gem of Italy is filled with historic architecture and art. It is an important walled city from the middle ages and you will want to linger here. Siena is a town to savor.

With limited time, here are a few suggestions for a rewarding visit. Choose what appeals to you and at a leisurely pace enjoy a taste of this medieval city.

➢ The Piazza del Campo. The square where the yearly Palio (bareback horse races) take place. Siena is divided into 17 districts (contrade). Since the 13th-century the districts fiercely compete at these races. Everything in Siena is in close proximity to the Piazza del Campo, one of the most beautiful

99

squares in Italy. It is the best place to experience Siena and start your day, sitting at one of the many cafés that line the Campo.

➤ The Museo Civico in the Palazzo Pubblico with its major frescoes by Ambrogio Lorenzetti and other early Sienese paintings. It faces the Campo and is open daily.

➤ For those who enjoy steep climbs, the Torre del Mangia (the name of an early bellringer) provides a breathtaking view of Siena and the Tuscan countryside. Also on the Campo. Open daily.

➤ The Duomo and the Duomo Museum with its Duccio Salon. Duccio was Siena's greatest painter. There is also a high catwalk for great views over Siena. Open daily.

➤ The 13th-century Basilica di San Domenico on a hillside behind St. Catherine's Sanctuary (Italy's patron saint). Another spot for great views. Open daily.

➤ The Pinocoteca Nazionale. The national picture gallery has 40 rooms filled with Sienese art from the 12th- to the 17th-century. (Don't try to visit every room on such a short stay.) Open daily.

➤ The Jewish synagogue, Via delle Scotte
14, Phone: 053-234-6654. Only open on
Sundays 10 am – 1 pm and 2 – 5 pm and
by prior booking for groups of 20 or
more. This late 18th-century building is
located in what was the ghetto where
Jews were forced to live by Cosimo 1st
in the 16th- century. I found it by wan-
dering these ancient alley-like lanes
looking for the outdoor Central Market,
which is right next to the synagogue.

➤ Enoteca Italiana Permanente (perma-
nent Italian library of wines), Fortezza
Medicea (follow signs), Phone: 0577-
288-497, Hours: Tuesdays–Saturday,
Noon–1 am. A great place to go for
wine tasting of some of Italy's best
wines. You can buy by the glass,
bottle or case.

➤ S. Maria dei Servi. The views from
the front steps and back terrace of
this Romanesque-Gothic church are
enough reason to stroll here. Follow
Via Salicotto.

The buses are from Sita, across from
the train station in Florence. They run
about every hour and cost under $10.
Take the bus that goes on the autostrada –
it's 30 minutes faster and the scenery
is basically the same. For the return

trip, you can buy your ticket at the
tobacco shop at the plaza where
you arrive.

➤ Reserve ahead for lunch at Antica
Trattoria "Papei," Piazza del Mercato 6,
Phone: 0577-280-894. Closed Monday.
You can eat at any restaurant that
catches your eye.

More-Timers
Panzano in Chianti

A 2 TO 3-DAY
FLORENTINE BREAK

Now that you have been overwhelmed
by Botticelli's "Primavera," admired
Michelangelo's "David" and the Medici
Chapel, fallen in love with Della Robbia's
beautiful circular tondos of infants and
Donatello's "Magdalene," walked the heels
off your shoes and bought enough new
leather accessories and jewelry to open a
boutique, how about a few days or even
weeks calmly exploring the beautiful
Tuscan hill towns and countryside? The
possibilities are endless. Follow your own
time, taste and budget.

You can rent simple rooms from families, apartments, farmhouses and even
luxurious villas with swimming pools and
servants as well as staying in charming
country inns and hotels scattered across
the whole region. Auto rentals are easily
arranged but automatic transmission cars
are double the price and hard to find.
Rentals should be arranged before leaving
the United States. If you choose to travel

by bus or train, check the schedules for
towns that you would like to visit. Fares
are nominal and often the country hotels
will pick you up at the local bus stop or
train station or arrange for a taxi.

Information on Tuscan accommodations
can be found at the Florence tourist
bureau, from guidebooks and travel articles, on the internet and from friends who
have enjoyed their visits to Tuscany. Some
popular destinations are Siena, Lucca,
Cortona, Arezzo, Greve, Castellina,
Panzano and S. Gimignano.

The following is a favorite of mine: a
few restful days in Panzano in Chianti,
which could easily be extended for even
greater enjoyment.

This is in an area of Tuscany that is
bursting with century-old vineyards and
olive farms. The whole region looks like a
lush landscape painting filled with cypress
groves, verdant farmland, rows of vines
and olive trees, all set in a gentle rolling
countryside. I reserved a room at Villa le
Barone, an ancient farm estate hotel of the
Della Robbia Family. After a short bus ride,
I arrived at the village square and called
the hotel from the bar. A member of the
staff graciously picked me up and brought
me to this serene heavenly spot where you
can hear country sounds of crickets,

singing birds, a farmer on his tractor and
children splashing in the pool.

I was shown to my room, which was not
in the main villa but a separate little guest
cottage. The simple cozy room had charming amenities like a tea kettle with packets
of tea and coffee and biscuits. I went
roaming the grounds, actually listening to
the quiet which was a soothing and welcome change.

I walked up to the old cemetery where
the view was even more spectacular and a
gentle breeze was blowing. I was definitely
in a collegiate Wordsworthian frame of
mind, spouting disconnected lines of poetry
and doing aerobic exercises at the same
time. Thank God no one was there to wit-
ness my performance and call the men in
white jackets (or whatever they are called
in Italy) to come and get me.

After coming back from the cemetery, I
walked around the estate to a terrace with
a lovely pool, garden and another spectacular vista. I ended my first afternoon's
odyssey in the antique-filled rear sitting
room that doubles as a bar and sat down
next to two French women. They told me
they also had discovered the hotel from
Karen Brown's *Guide of Charming Italian
Country Inns* and were as delighted as I
was with this elegant farm hotel.

I experienced three wonderful days
where I swam, read, walked country roads,
visited the local market (bought gold slippers for $5 – my friends call them Lynn's
Italian hooker shoes), ate wonderful country Tuscan cooking accompanied by very
drinkable Chianti wines and chatted with a
friendly assortment of international guests
in a melange of languages (including my
limited but useful school French). My
three-day visit came to an end, and I said
my arrivedercis to the Villa le Barone, a
place of nurturing serenity that will
remain with me as a cherished memory.

➤ **VILLA LE BARONE, Via S. Leolino
19, 50020, Panzano in Chianti
(31 km. South of Florence).
Phone: 055-85261, Fax: 055-852277,
Single: 195,000 lira ($95), Double:
390,000-500,000 lira ($195-$250),
includes breakfast and dinner.** In
Panzano, visit Dario, the most elegant
butcher shop and considered to be the
Tiffany of meats and gourmet delicacies
by Florentine chefs and gourmands.

Basta!
(Enough)

In the Essentials chapter of this guide I mention how important it is to know the Italian sentence for: "I do not speak Italian." However, I neglected to mention the word *"enough"*–basta.

Before my first trip to Italy, I called a friend, an Italian priest, to inquire where his family lived in Italy. I told him I had no set itinerary but perhaps I would stop by to visit. Father "M" gave me his cousin's name and address (who spoke a little English) in Nocera Umbria but said it was way off the beaten tourist path and difficult to find. Of course that was the wrong thing to say to someone who adores challenges as well as "off- the-beaten-path destinations."

It took me several bus and train changes but I arrived at 11:45 am in the village square. I walked into the café and pulled out my slip of paper with the cousin's name. With a bit of pantomime the owner

understood I was looking for the family
of Padre M. Obviously this gentleman was
really impressed that I was an American
friend of Padre M. He took me by the
hand back to the far side of the square
while speaking very loudly to me and
gestured to the left–holding up three
fingers. I thanked him profusely and
followed his directions, walking to the
third street (lugging my valise which
today is one quarter of the size).

Now I stood on the corner of a residential street not knowing whether to turn
right or left and looked for someone to
help me. I saw two young boys playing
ball in the middle of the street. I walked
up to them and again pulled out my piece
of paper. One of the youngsters started
shouting and pointing to the house
directly behind him. Both boys helped
me carry the heavy suitcase up the
steps of the house.

Out of a side room came running a tiny,
very elderly lady. I showed her the card
with Father M's name and his cousin's
name. She hugged me and brought me
right into the dining room and propelled
me to a chair, chatting on and on in Italian
and saying Padre M's name over and over.

With pantomime, I discovered the
cousins were away on vacation and she

(Julia) did not speak English and was the aunt or another cousin of Padre M. I was her most honored and distinguished guest from America. She left me with the two boys who were rapidly talking to me in Italian. I understood "America" and "Padre M" and somehow, because I knew him, I must indeed be a very important person.

Julia returned in less than five minutes with a large cake, a pot of coffee and a pot of tea. I gestured to the tea and she then proceeded to serve me a huge slice of cake. I thanked her and dutifully ate my cake and drank my tea. As soon as I was finished, she cut me another slice. I again said thank you, "Grazie" and struggled to eat this second serving. Julia kept saying "Mangia!" and gesturing to eat, so I ate.

Now I was really stuffed to the gills! Julia then gets up and sends me off with the boys. I quickly learned I was being taken back to the center of town to the butcher and the baker and introduced to everyone as the "Americana" friend of Padre M. They were all excited to meet me. I guess coming all the way from America and being a friend of a loved priest from this town was very special.

We returned to Julia's house where she had lunch on the table, including an enormous bowl of pasta, in less than an hour. Every time Julia refilled my plate with pasta I said "Grazie" and Julia beamed. I did not know how to get her to stop serving me without insulting her hospitality. Finally, before I exploded I showed my watch and pantomimed it was time for the train.

The boys walked me (they almost had to roll me – I was like a stuffed goose ready for a pate) back to the station where I boarded the very next train.

If someone had only taught me "basta" as well as "non parlo." I might have had just one refill of pasta and said "basta pasta" and Julia would have understood. No matter, it was a wonderful day – basta!

–*Lynn Portnoy*

RESOURCES

To maximize your enjoyment of the fabulous artistic treasures, I recommend a bit of reading before your trip as well as the selection of a good guidebook to take with you when visiting the churches and museums. Here are a few good choices:

BOOKS

Michelin – Green Guide for Tuscany, small and easy to carry – filled with great information.

The Blue Guide – Florence, highly informative cultural guide.

The Heritage Guide – Florence by Touring Club of Italy, with great detailed information on the Renaissance masterpieces, readable maps and light enough to carry with you. I highly recommend taking this, Michelin or the Blue Guide along with *Going Like Lynn- Florence*.

RESOURCES

Insight Compact Guides – Florence, a handy small book with general information. *Access Guide – Florence and Venice*, Richard Saul Wurman, interesting detailed color-coded information by neighborhoods of hotels, restaurants, shops and attractions, plus historical trivia. A bit larger but still possible to carry with you or copy the sightseeing pages of interest to you. I enjoy the suggestions from Florentines about their favorite places.

Frommers Italy, good general guidebook. Read chapter on Florence and take notes – too heavy to carry with you.

The Companion Guide to Florence by Eve Borsook, Companion Guides Woodbridge U.K., and Badell Brewer, Rochester, NY, a wonderful reference book for serious students of the Renaissance.

RESOURCES

History of Italian Renaissance Art, Frederick Hartt, edited by David Wilkins, 4th Edition, Abrams, New York, a beautifully illustrated book of Renaissance painting, sculpture and architecture. A special book for those with a passion for Renaissance art.

My old school books: *Lives of the Artists – Vasari and History of Italian Renaissance Art* by Bernard Berenson.

Under the Tuscan Sun and *Bella Tuscany*, by Frances Mayes. Two delightful books by an American living part-time in Tuscany.

TOURIST OFFICES

In the United States:

New York: 630 5th Avenue, Suite 1565, New York, NY 10011. Phone: 212-245-5618, Fax: 212-586-9249. Email: enitny@italiantourism.com

RESOURCES

Chicago: 500 N. Michigan Avenue, Suite 2240, Chicago, IL 60611. Phone: 312-644-0996, Fax: 312-644-3019. Email: enitch@italiantourism.com

Los Angeles: 12400 Wilshire Blvd., Suite 550, Los Angeles, CA 90025. Phone: 310-820-2977, Fax: 310-820-6357. Email: enitla@earthlink.net

Florence:
Visitors Information Office: (Informazione turistica) in the train station or at Via Camillo Cavour 1r (between Via dei Gori and Via Guelfa), Phone: 055-290-832/3, Fax: 055-276-0383 Monday – Saturday 8:15am 7:15pm; Sunday 8:15am – 1:45pm March – October.
Remainder of the year:
8:15am – 1:45pm Monday – Saturday.

There is another office at Borgo Santa Croce 29r (behind Piazza Santa Croce), Phone: 055-234-0444. Monday–Saturday 8:15am – 7:15pm. They close for long lunches so call for exact hours.

RESOURCES

ONLINE

Rail information, timetables and ticket prices: www.raileurop.com

General information on arts, entertainment, restaurants, hotels, shopping and sports: www.italytour.com (they also have photos)

Monthly listings of recommendations for art museums, galleries, wineries as well as hotels, restaurants and other sightseeing ideas: www.itwg.com

Listings on current cultural events, restaurants, as well as museum and monument maps of Florence: www.florence.net/eng/

A good informational site with interesting extras, such as: "hidden corners of Florence", markets and historical shops – as well as listings of theatres, events and ticket information: www.tiac.net/users/pendini/

RESOURCES

MUSEUM TICKETS

Essential to reserve ahead for Uffizi, Accademia, Medici Chapel and Pitti Palace.
Phone: 011-39-055-294-883

City Museums (Buy in Florence at any city museum) – Florentine Museum Booklet, 10,000 lire. Gives you a 50 percent discount on selected museums including Brancacci Chapel and Palazzo Vecchio.

PERFORMANCE TICKETS

Teatro Comunale, Corso Italia 12 (at Via Magenta), Phone: 011-39-055-211158. Symphony, opera and ballet performances. You don't need the most expensive tickets. The theatre is not huge and seats in the second tier are fine. Also check the magazine **Florence Concierge** for music or dance performance schedule of all Florentine theatres and churches.

RESOURCES

CURRENCY EXCHANGE

Before you go, purchase at least $100 of lire or after January, 2002, the new currency Euros. On your trip  there are ATMs called Bancomat all over Florence (be sure you have a PIN number for each bank card). Other choices – American Express, banks and currency exchange windows.

TRAIN SCHEDULES and PRICES

In the United States: call Rail Europe: 1-800-438-7245

CAR RENTALS

U.S. Office:

Avis, phone: 800-331-2112,

Budget, phone: 800-472-3325,

Hertz, phone: 800-654-3001,

Auto Europe, phone: 800-223-5555

RESOURCES

BUS TICKETS

Valid for 1 hour
to 3-day passes
(1,500 lire to 11,000
lire–75 cents to $5.50). Purchase tick-
ets at bus station or tobacco shops.

Linee Ecologiche–a minibus that
shuttles tourists to all of the important
churches and museums. There are five
routes – A, B, C, D, P - differentiated
by color on the ATAF Bus Map. *In
Florence, check at bus stations for
current schedules.*

WALKING TOURS

**The Original and Best Walking
Tour of Florence,** Piazza S. Stefano
#2r. Phone: 011-39-055-264-5033 or
011-39-329-613-2730.
Email: walkingtours@artviva.com
Internet: www.artviva.com. Their
most popular tour is called "The

RESOURCES

Original Florence Walk" and costs
40,000 lire (about $20) per person con-
ducted by lively tour guides in small
groups. Visit the Duomo, S. Trinita,
Orsanmichele, Baptistry, Bell Tower,
Piazza della Signoria, Piazza del
Repubblica, Ponte Vecchio plus shop-
ping streets in the historic district.
Other walking tours by the same
company are: Mornings in Tuscany,
Highlights of the Uffizi Gallery, the
Best of Tuscany.

The Accidental Tourist.
Phone: 011-39 055-699-376
Fax: 055/699048,
Email: info@accidentaltourist.com,
Internet: www.accidentaltourist.com
Has a tour called *"A Perfect Day in
the Chianti Countryside."* Ride a bike
or walk through the Chianti country-
side in small groups and end with a
Tuscan meal.

RESOURCES

PRIVATE GUIDES

Inquire at Tourist Bureau, your travel
agent, hotel or friends for names of
private guides (about $150-350 a day).

PRIVATE LECTURES

A special private lecture on
Renaissance history and tour of
important Renaissance sites by Frank
Peters, an American historian who
works part time as a concierge at the
charming Morondi alla Crocetta Hotel
and gives an excellent three-hour
combination lecture and tour.
Reasonably priced.
Phone: 011-39-055-234-4747
Fax: 011-39-055-248-0954.

RESOURCES

PHARMACY

The pharmacy inside Santa Maria Novella Staion. They speak some English and are open all night, Phone: 055-216-761 Remember to have your prescriptions labeled with generic name and dosage as well as written down in your pocket notebook.)

UNITED STATES CONSULATE

Lungarno Amerigo Vespucci 38, Phone: 055-239-8276 *for serious problems.*

EMERGENCY NUMBERS

Ambulance, Phone: 055-118-394

Police, Phone: 113.

Going like Lynn©

A Series of Liberating
Travel Primers for Women

For information on how to book
Lynn Portnoy as a speaker at your next
women's function, call toll free:
1-888-386-9688

Or visit lynn on the internet:

goinglikelynn.com
email: info@goinglikelynn.com

For book orders, please use the
order form on the following pages.

Going like Lynn

A Liberating Series of Travel Guide Books for Women

Going like Lynn–Florence
$14.95 plus $2.75 shipping & handling
($17.70 total). *Add $1.10 shipping & handling
for each additional copy.*

Going like Lynn–Paris
$12.95 plus $2.75 shipping & handling
($15.70 total). *Add $1.10 shipping & handling
for each additional copy.*

Going like Lynn–New York
$13.95 plus $2.75 shipping & handling
($16.70 total). *Add $1.10 shipping & handling
for each additional copy.*

Special Purchase: Going like Lynn–Florence, New York and Paris (Set of three)
$35 plus $4.00 shipping & handling
($39.00 total). *Add $3.00 shipping & handling
for each additional set.*